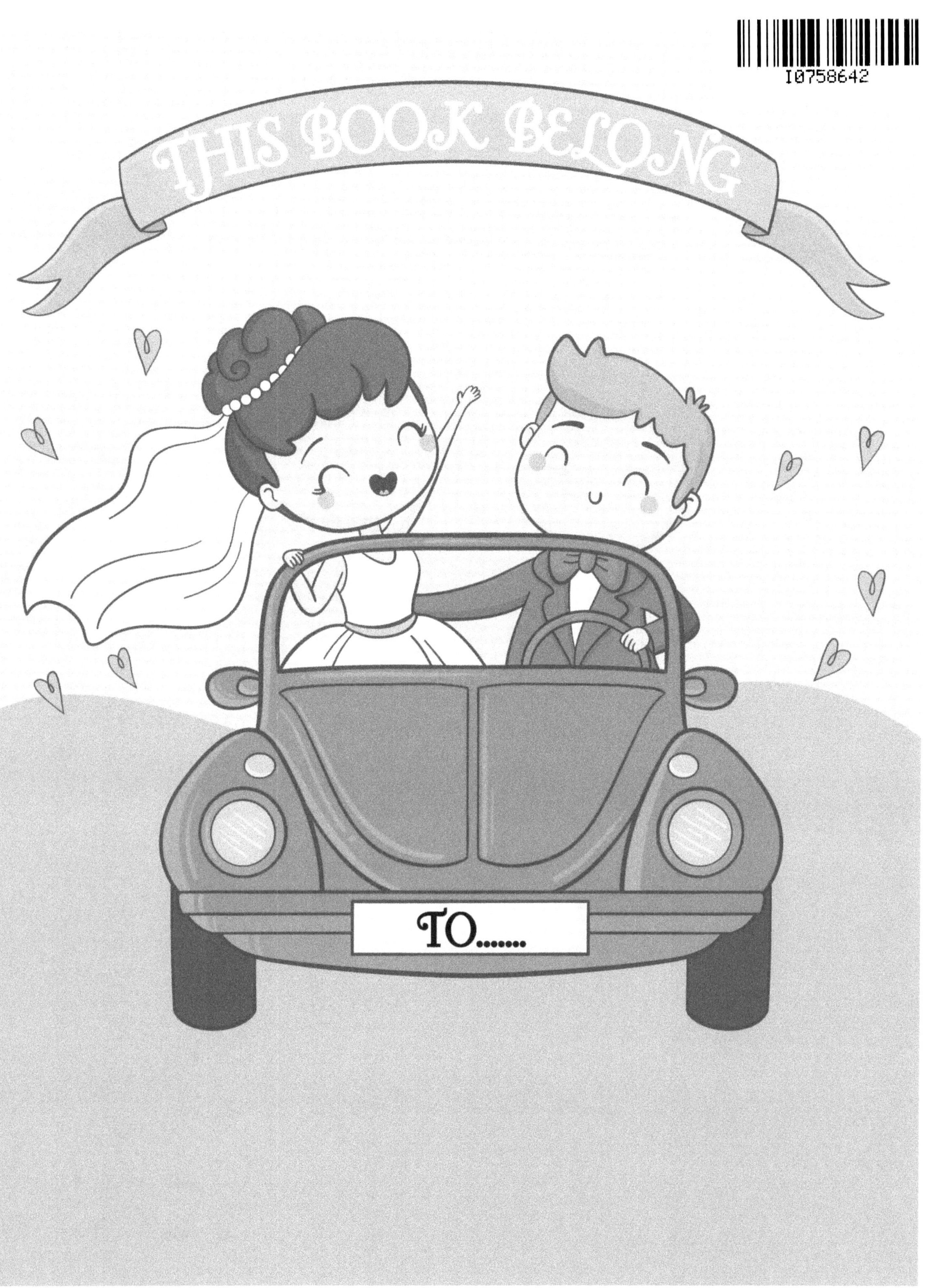

I0758642
THIS BOOK BELONG
TO........

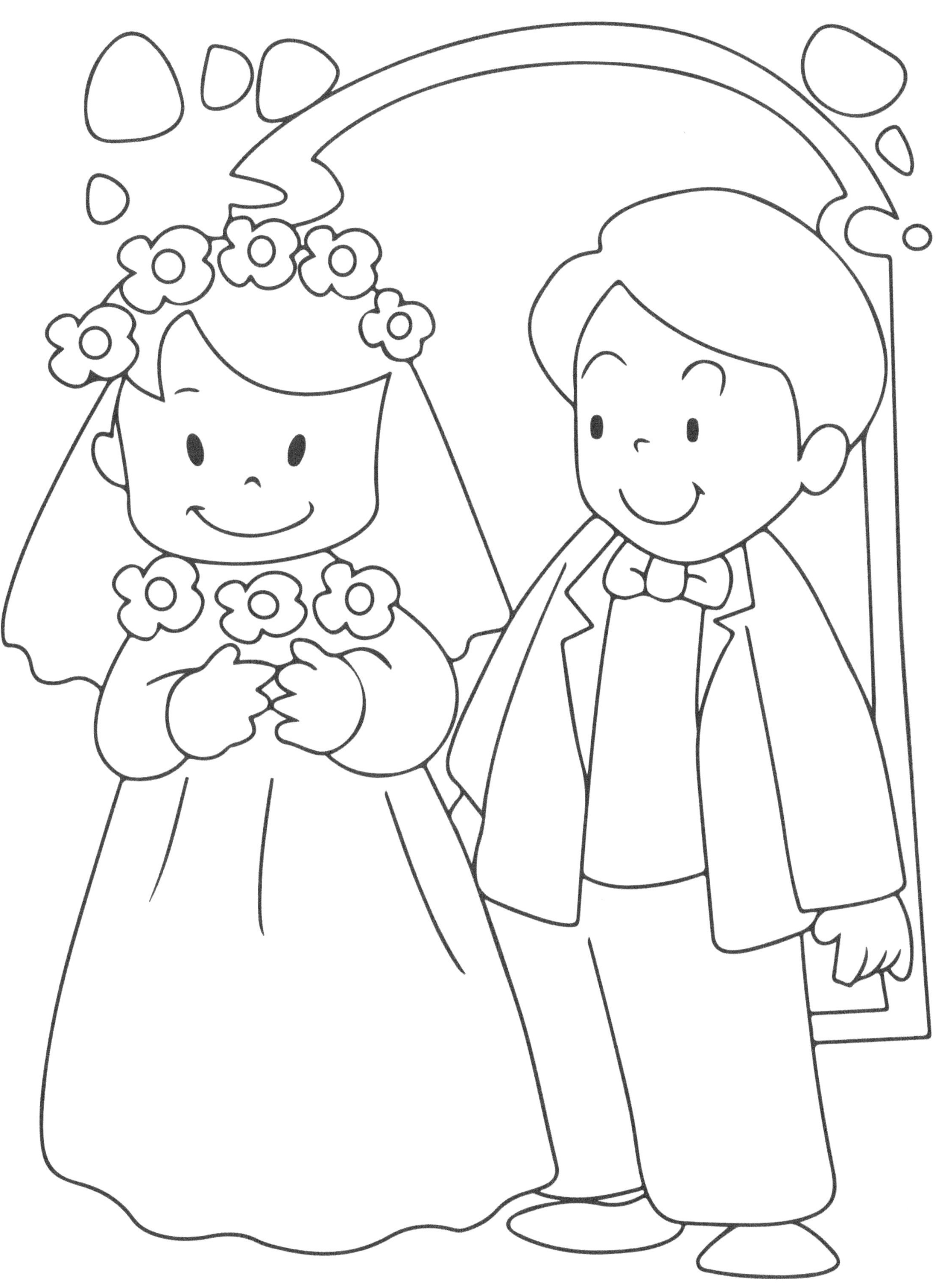

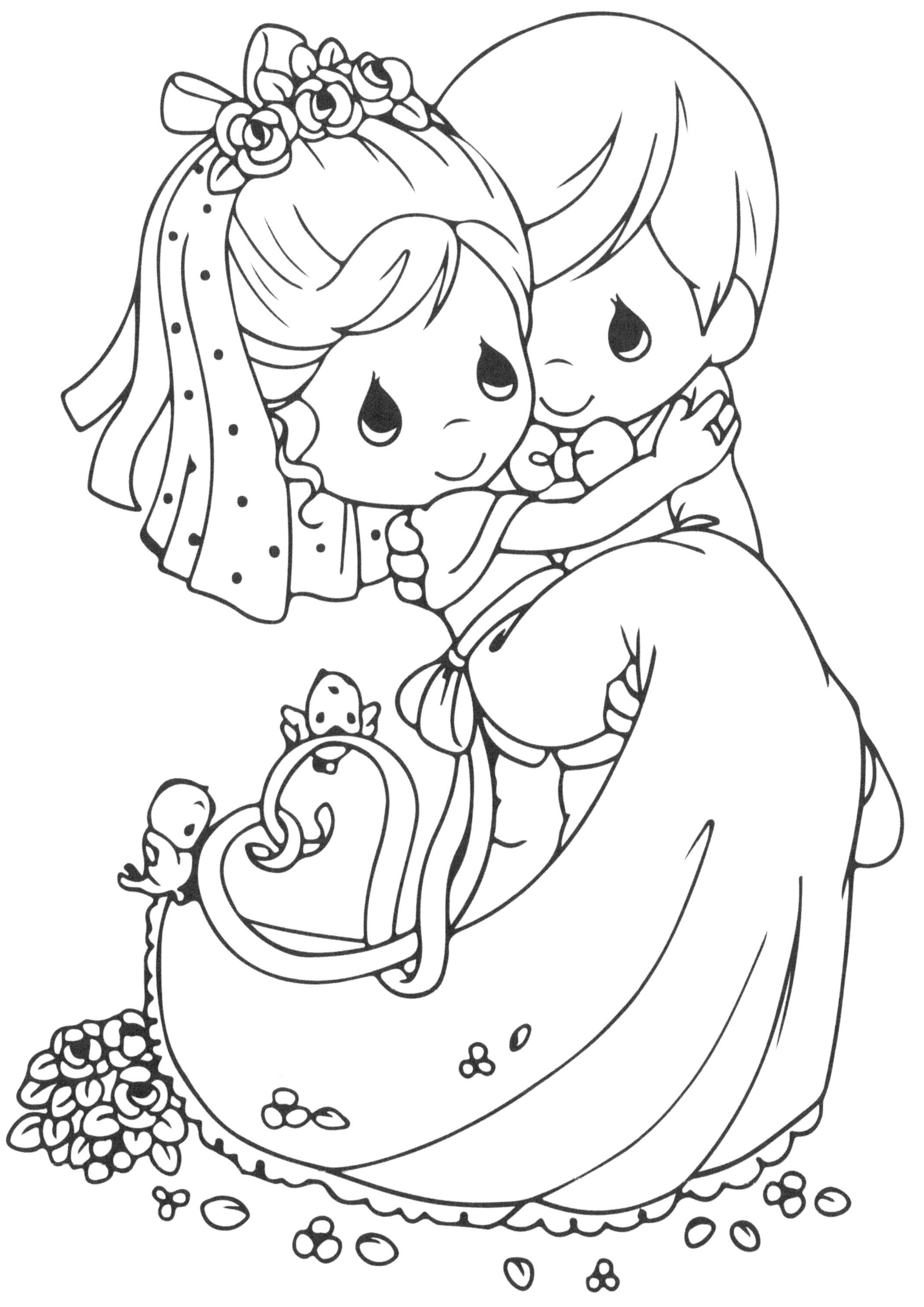

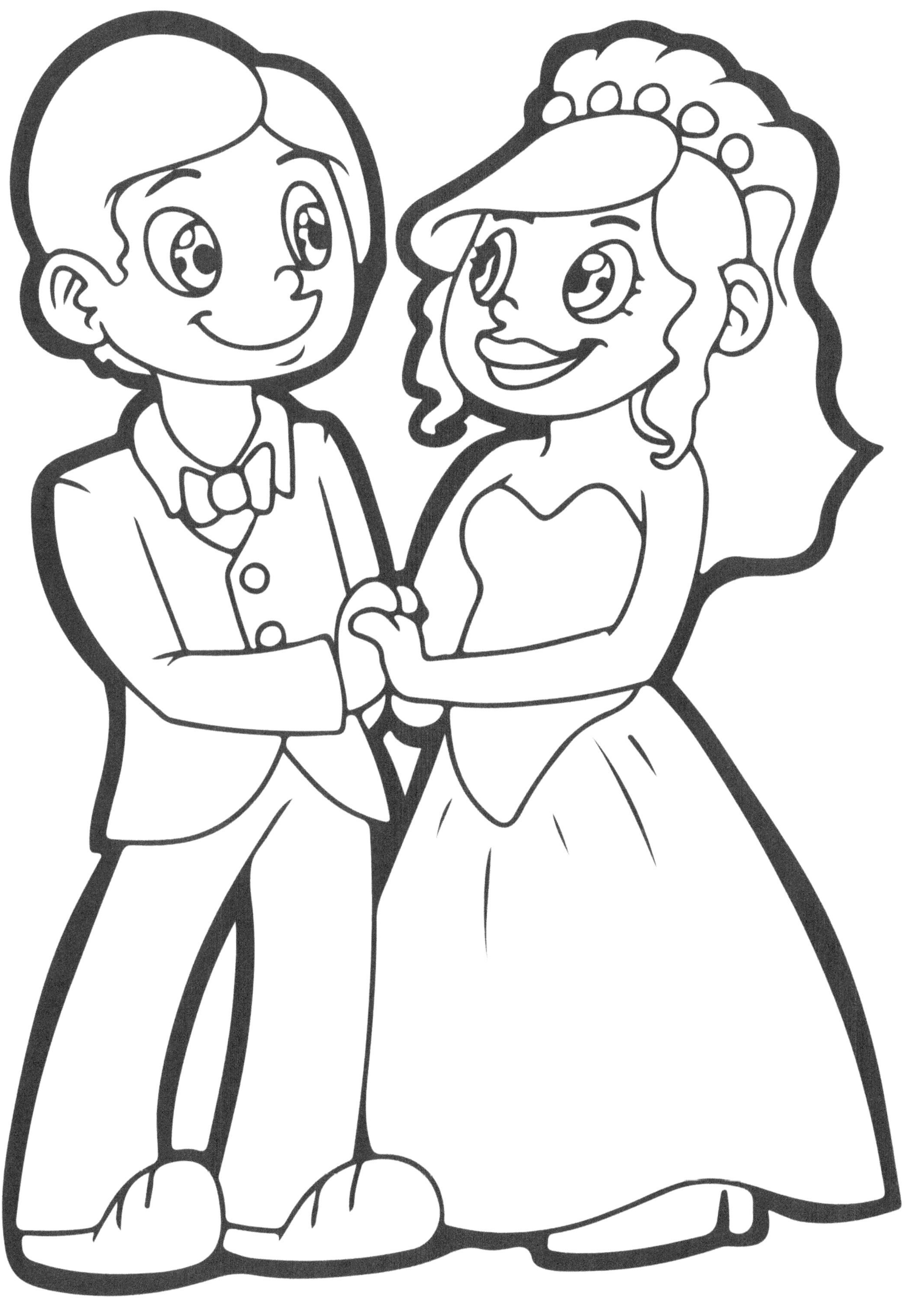

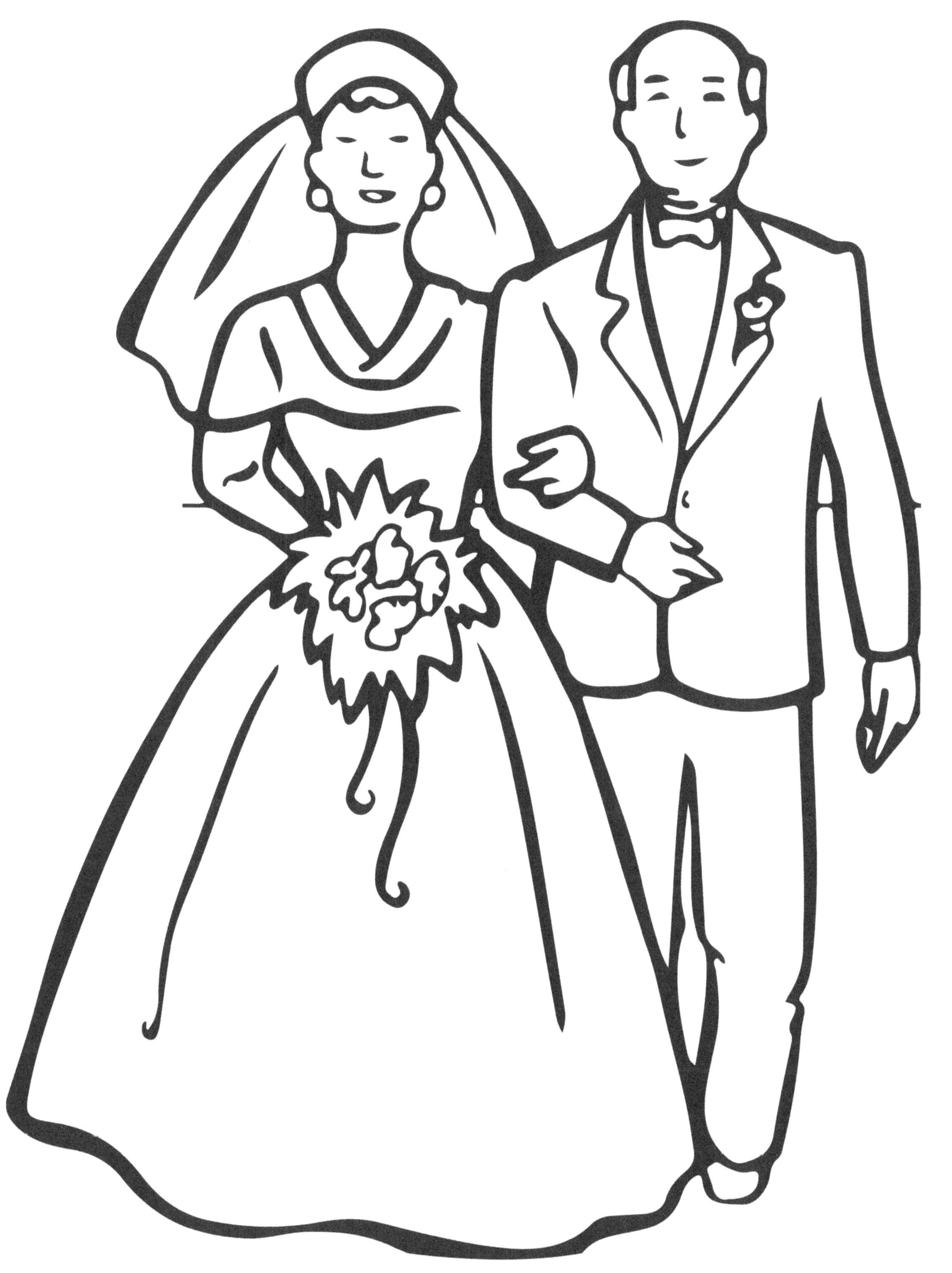

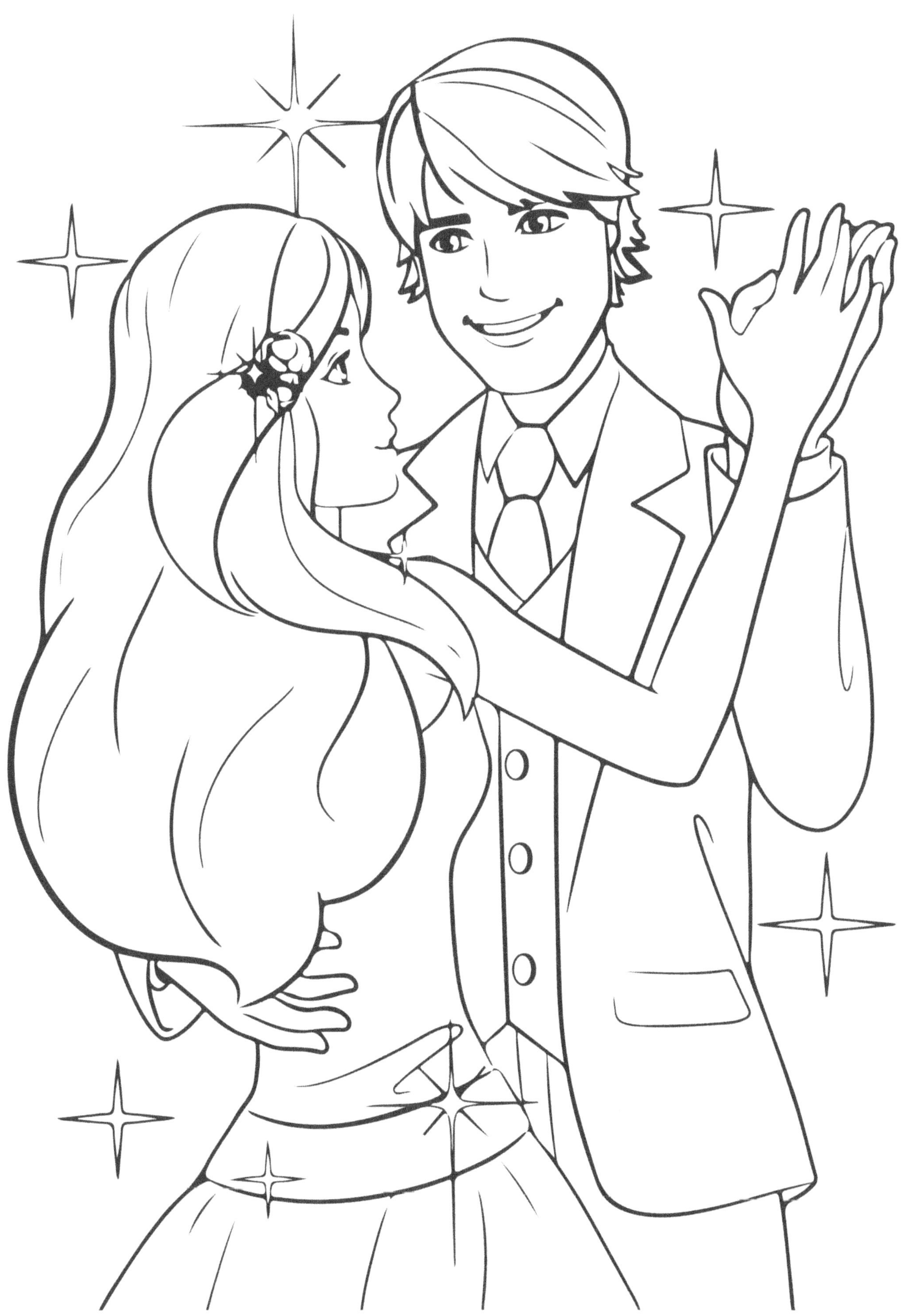

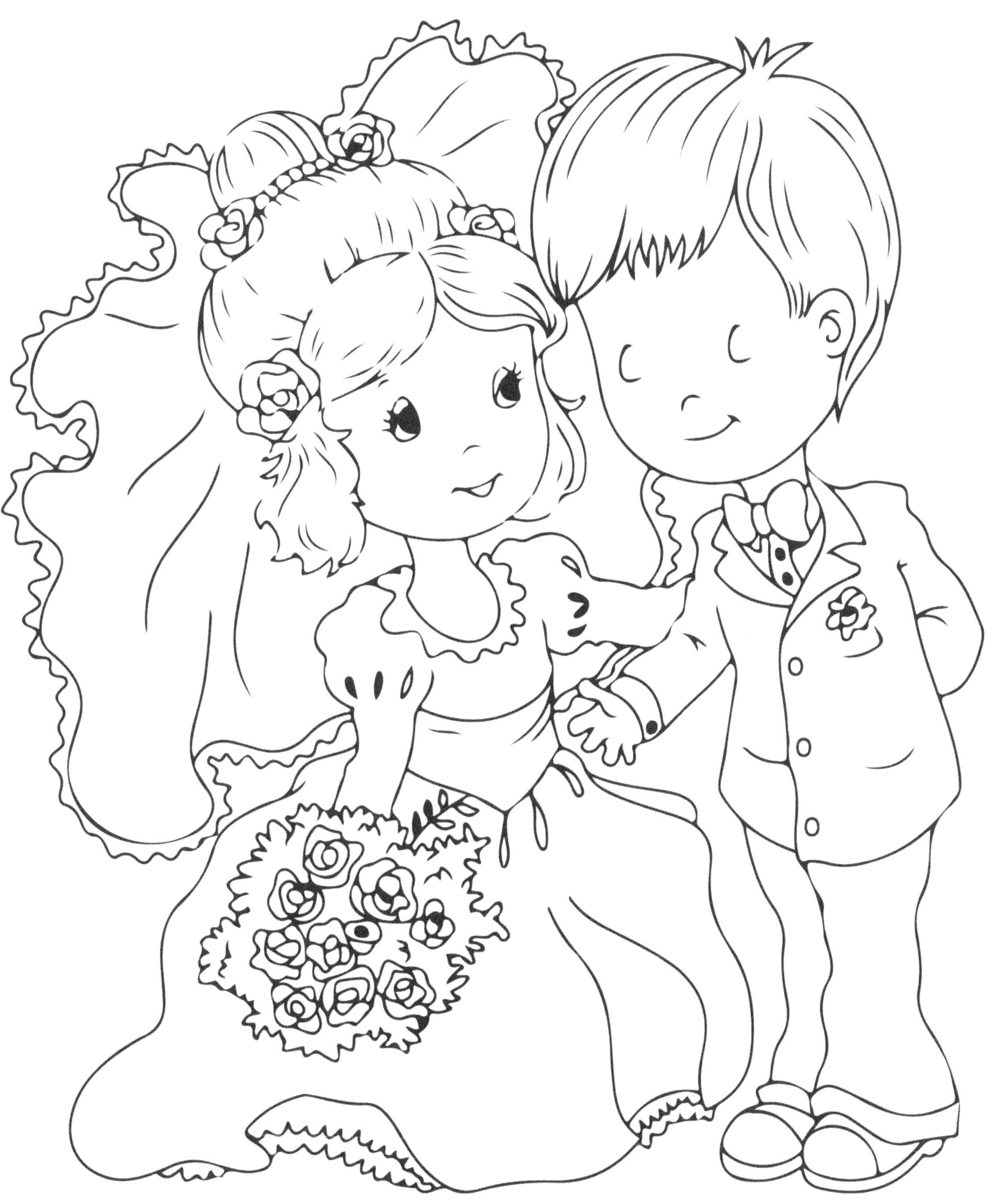

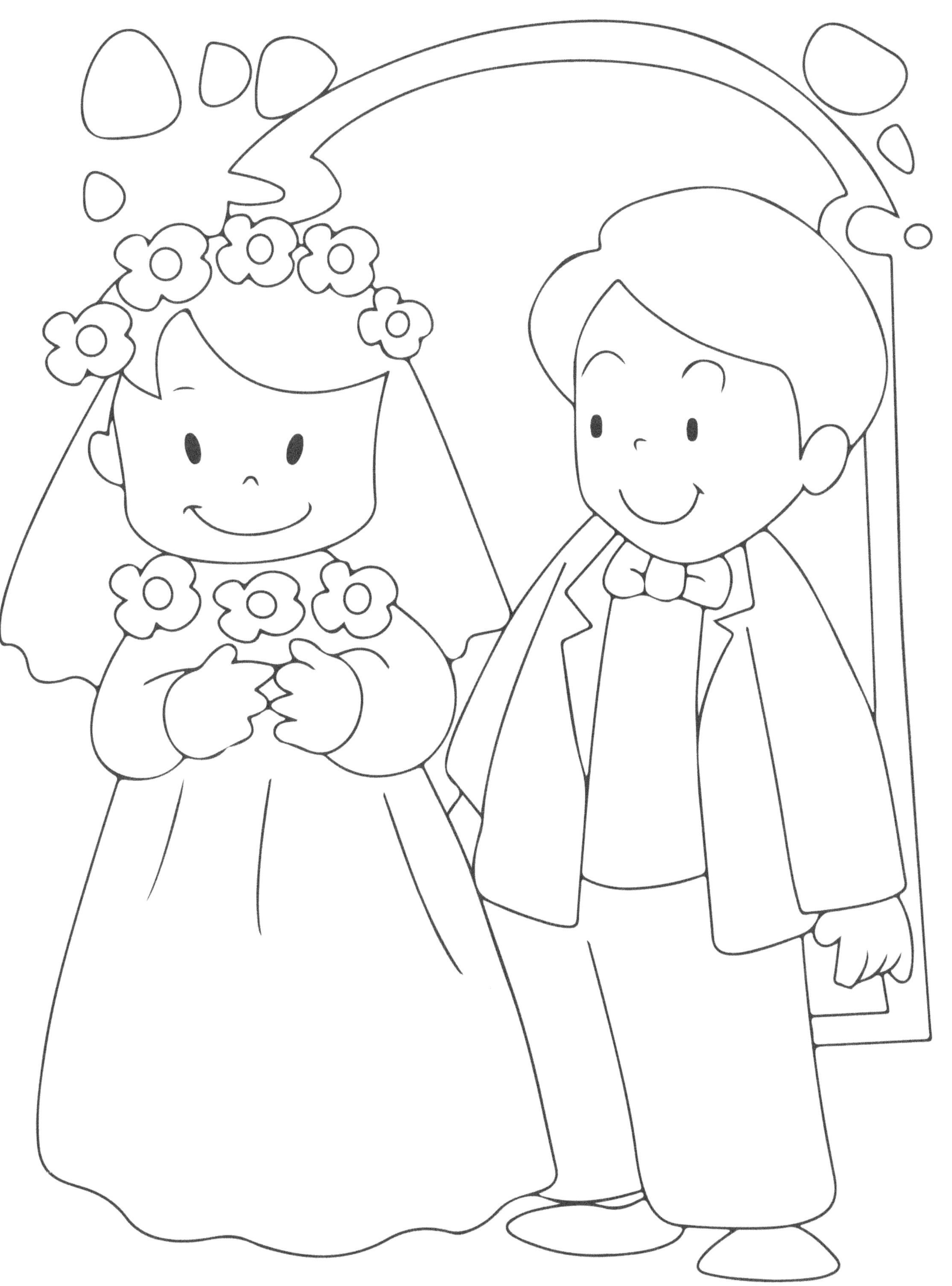

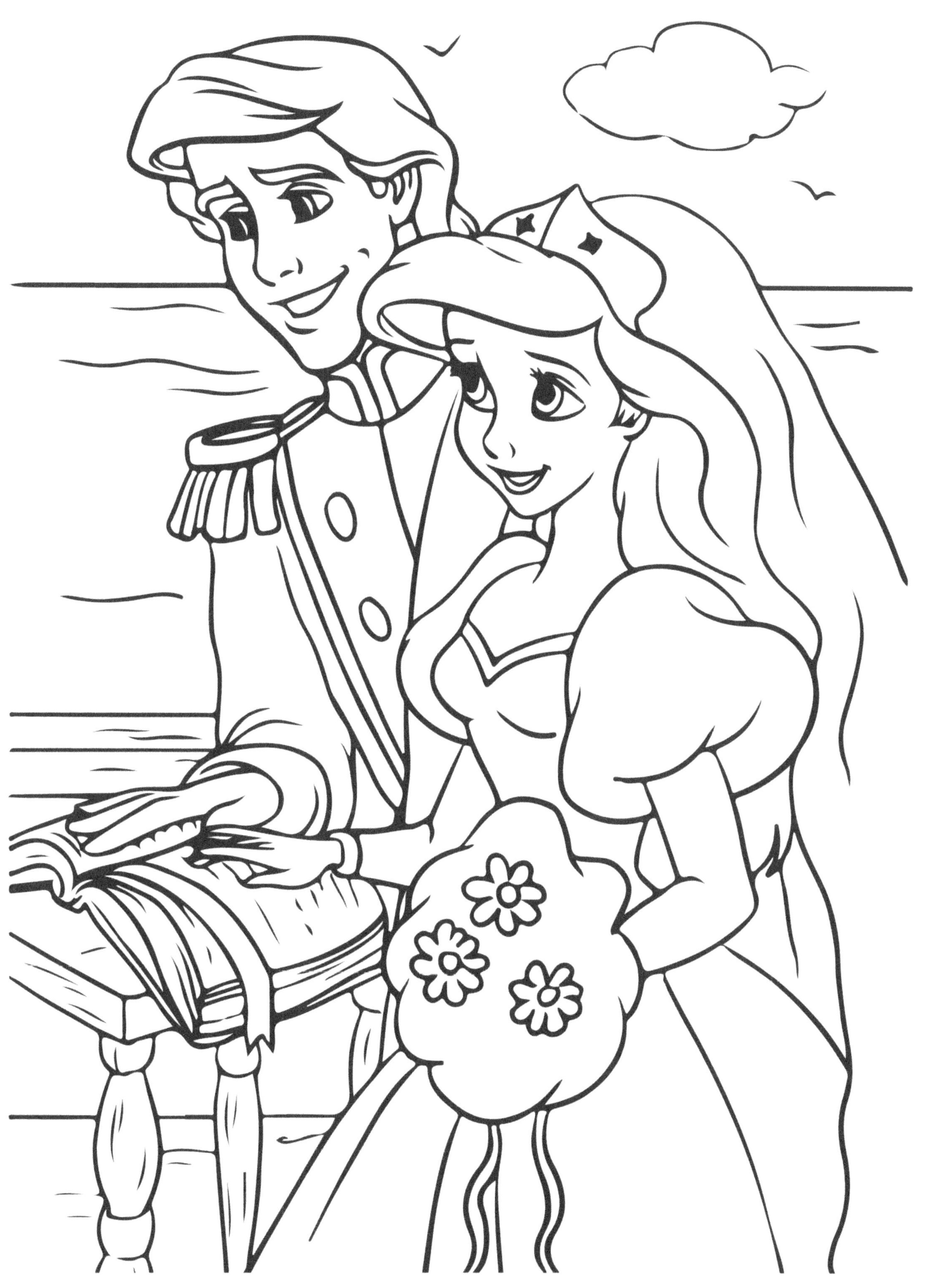

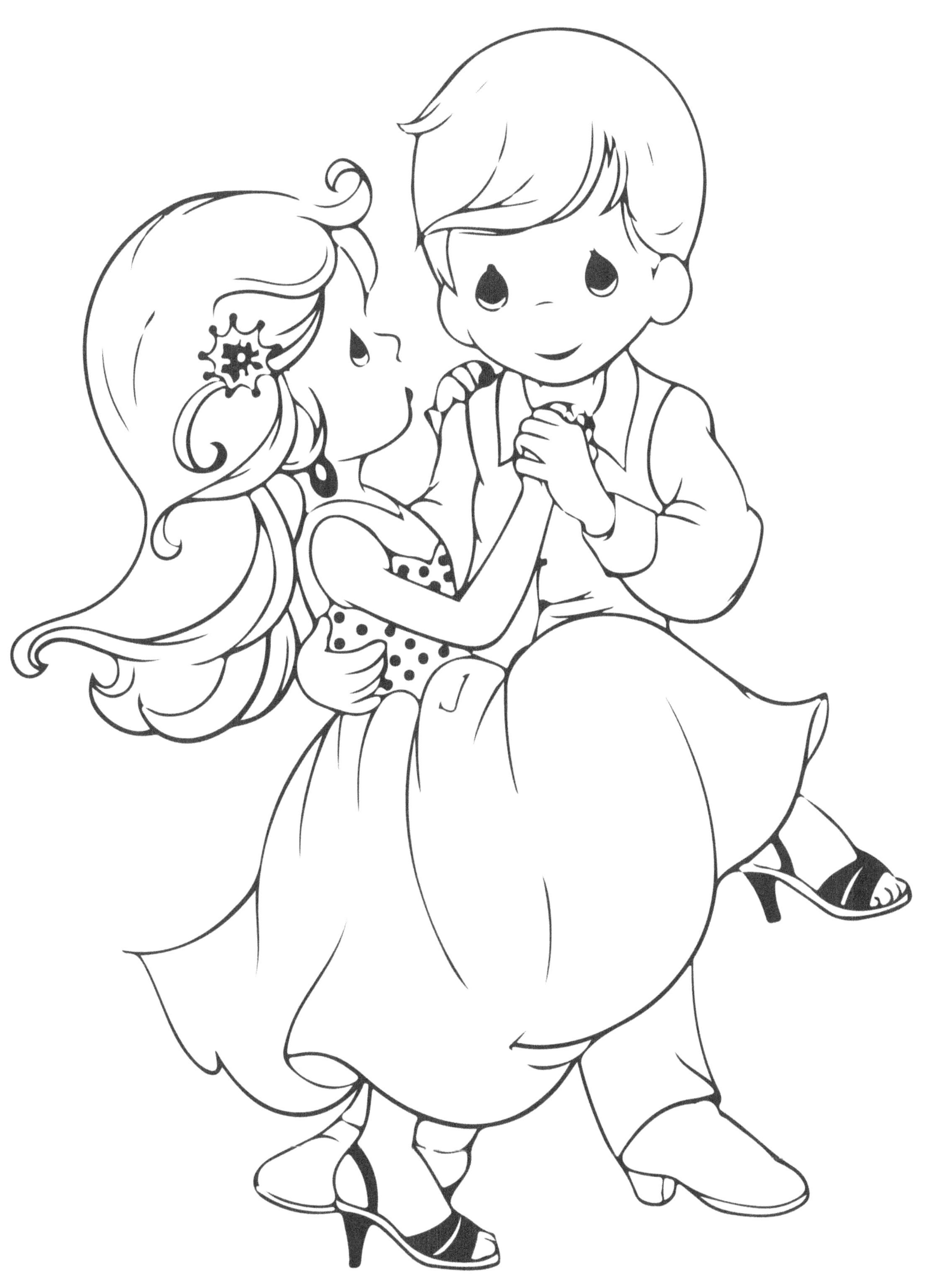

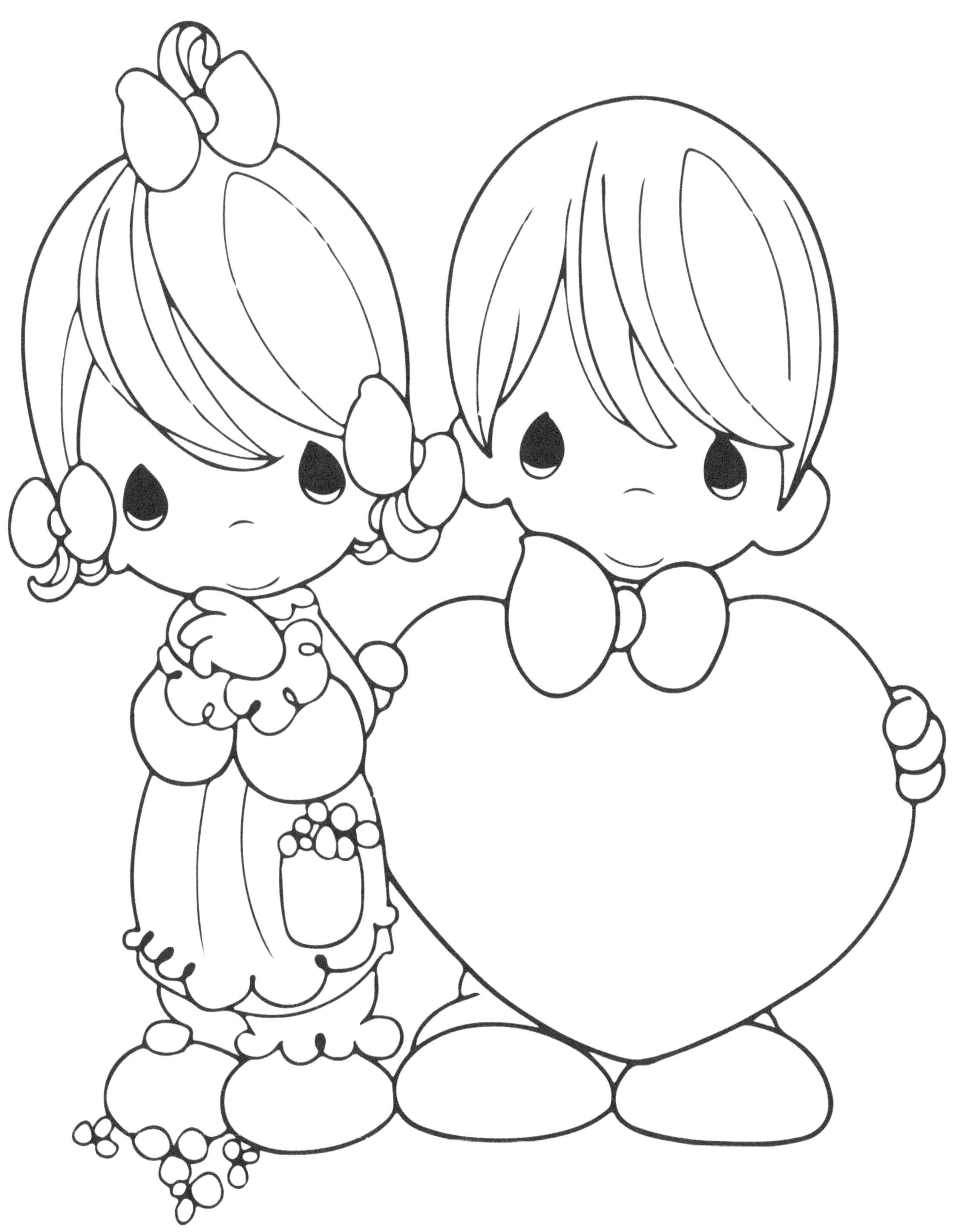

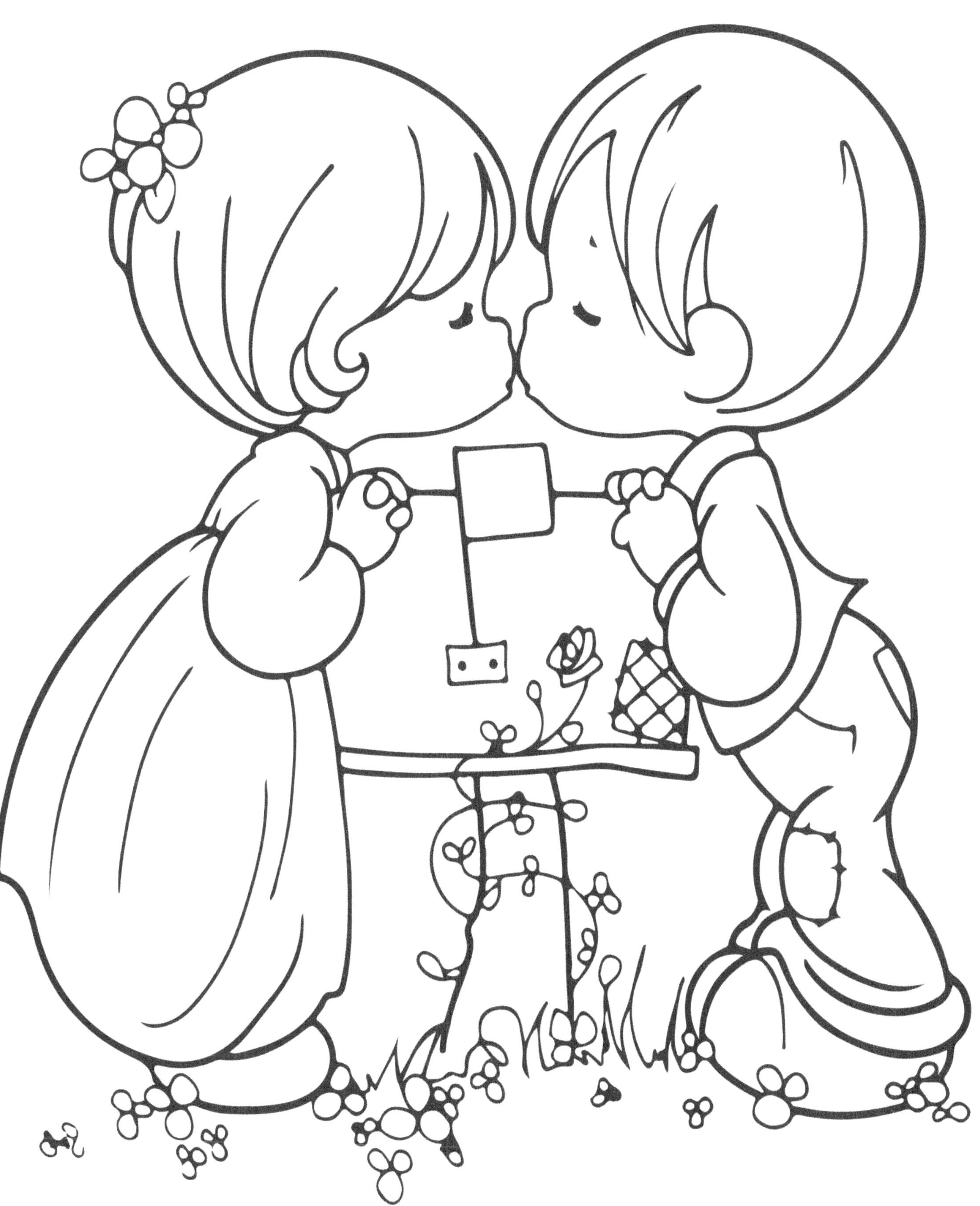

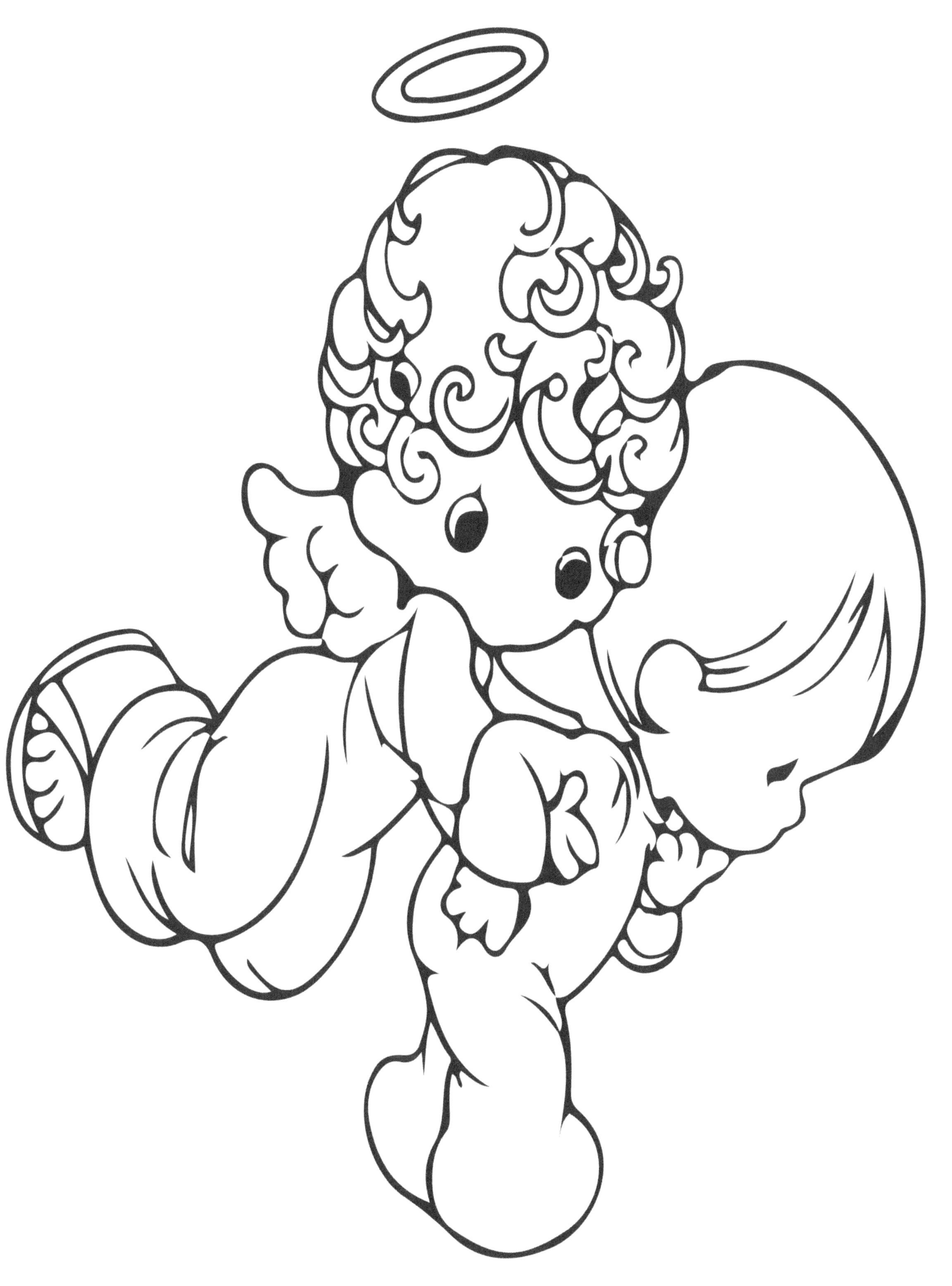

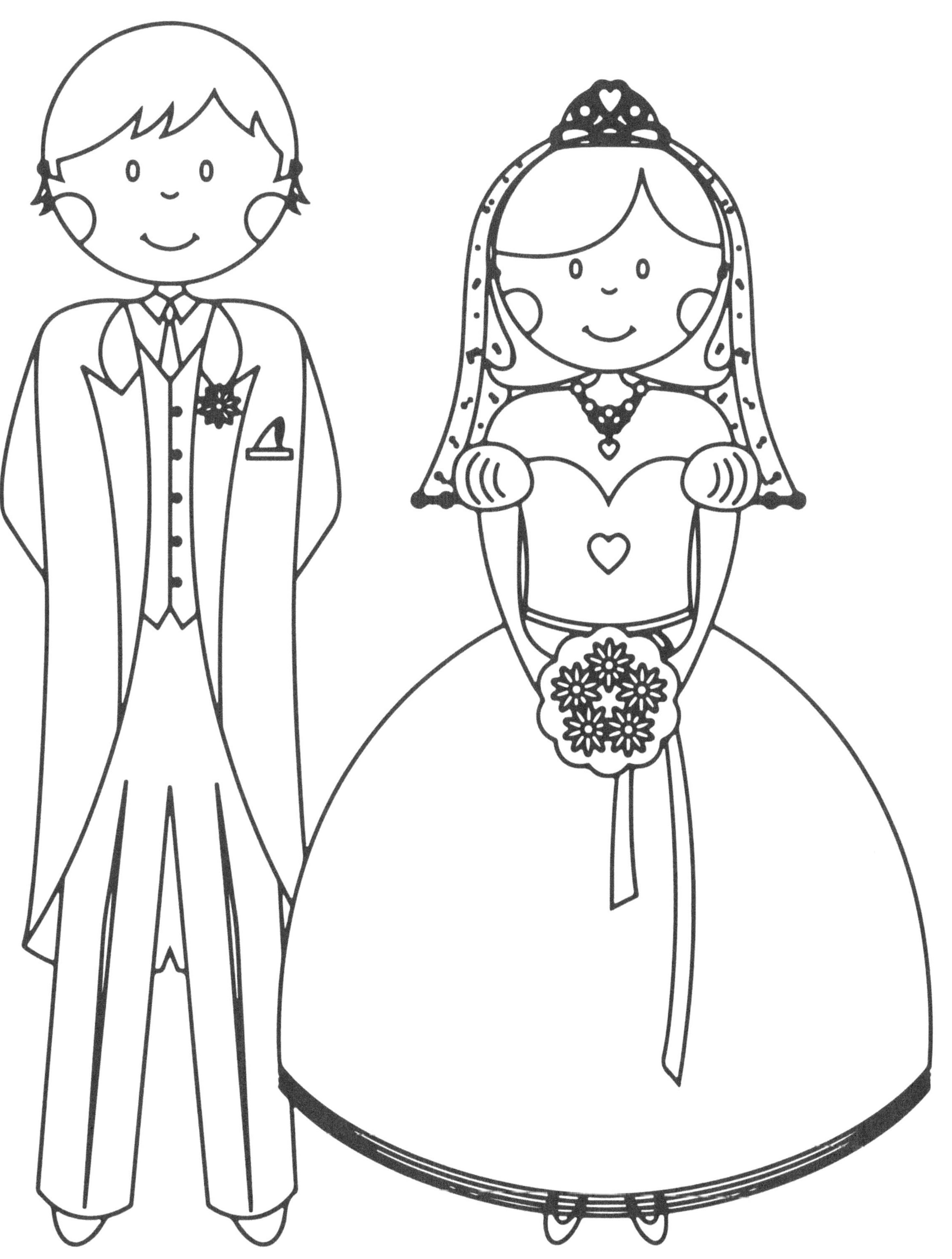

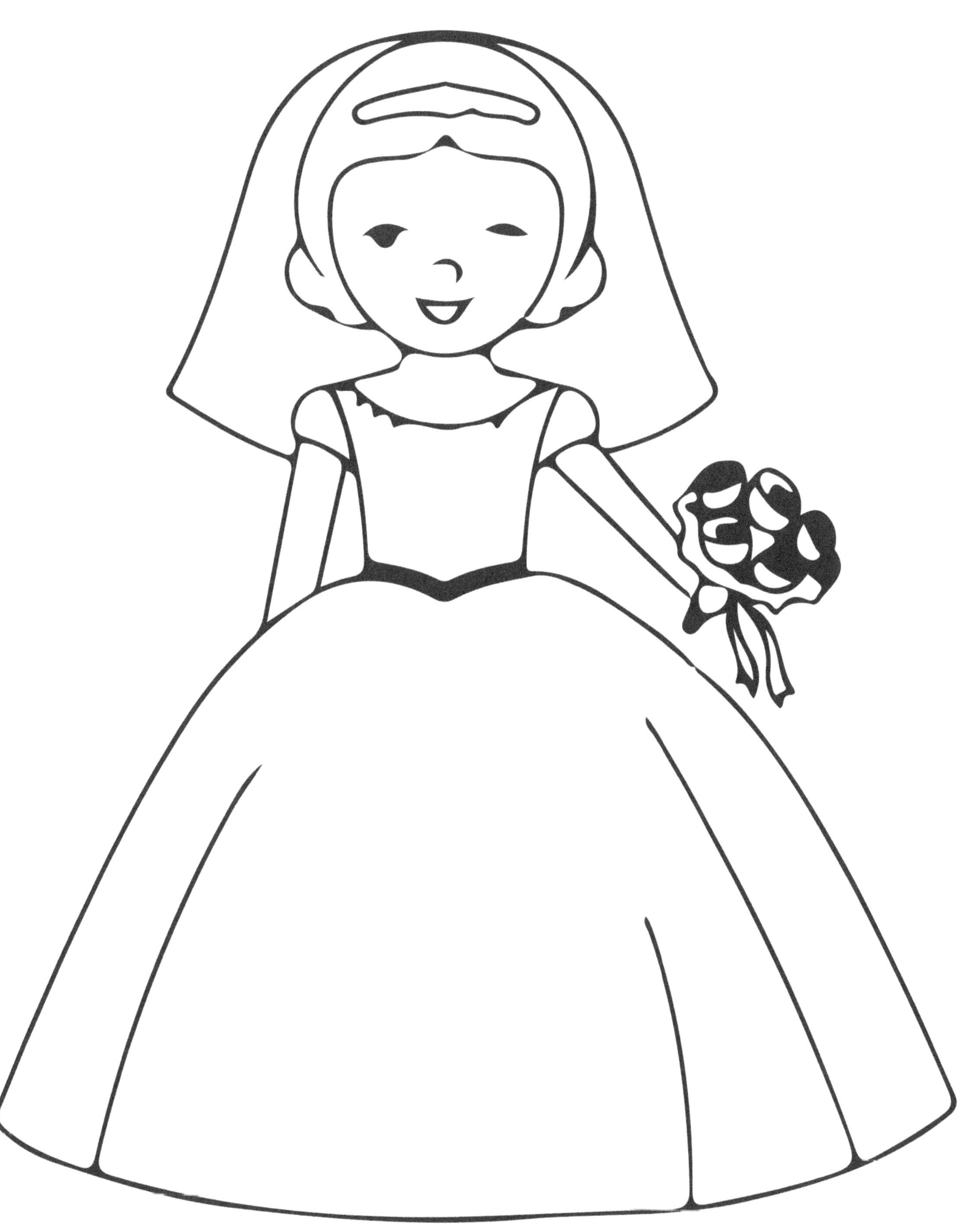

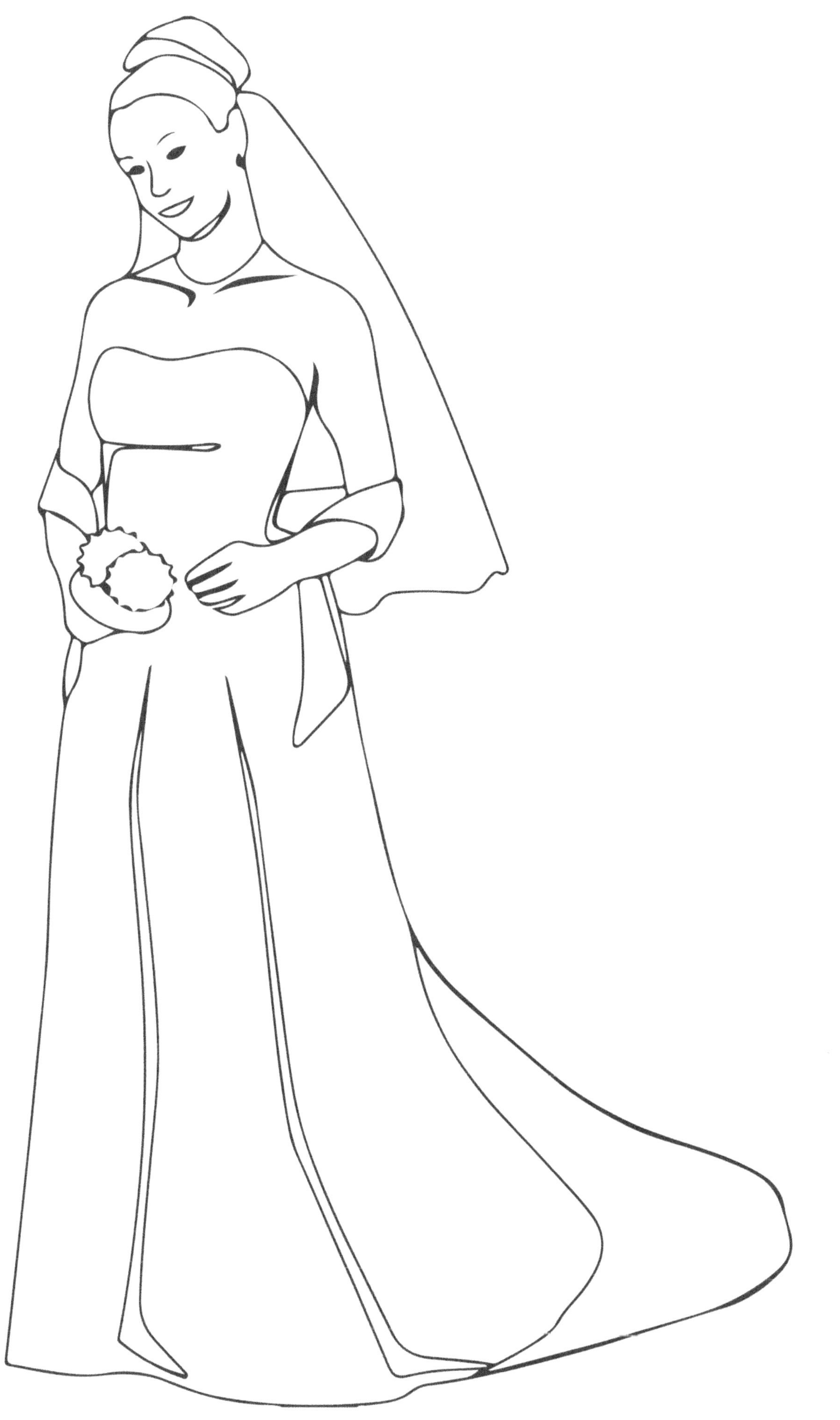

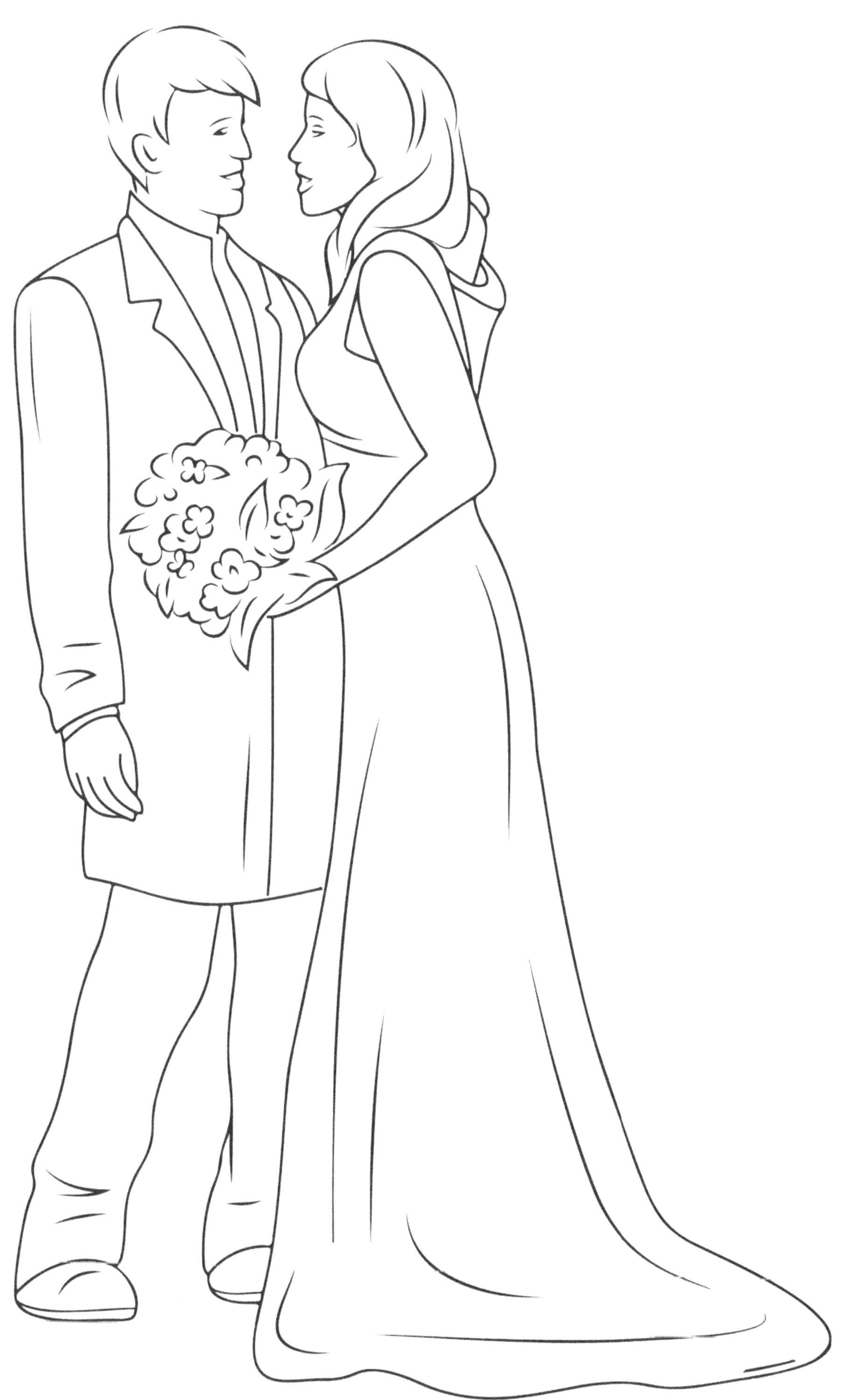

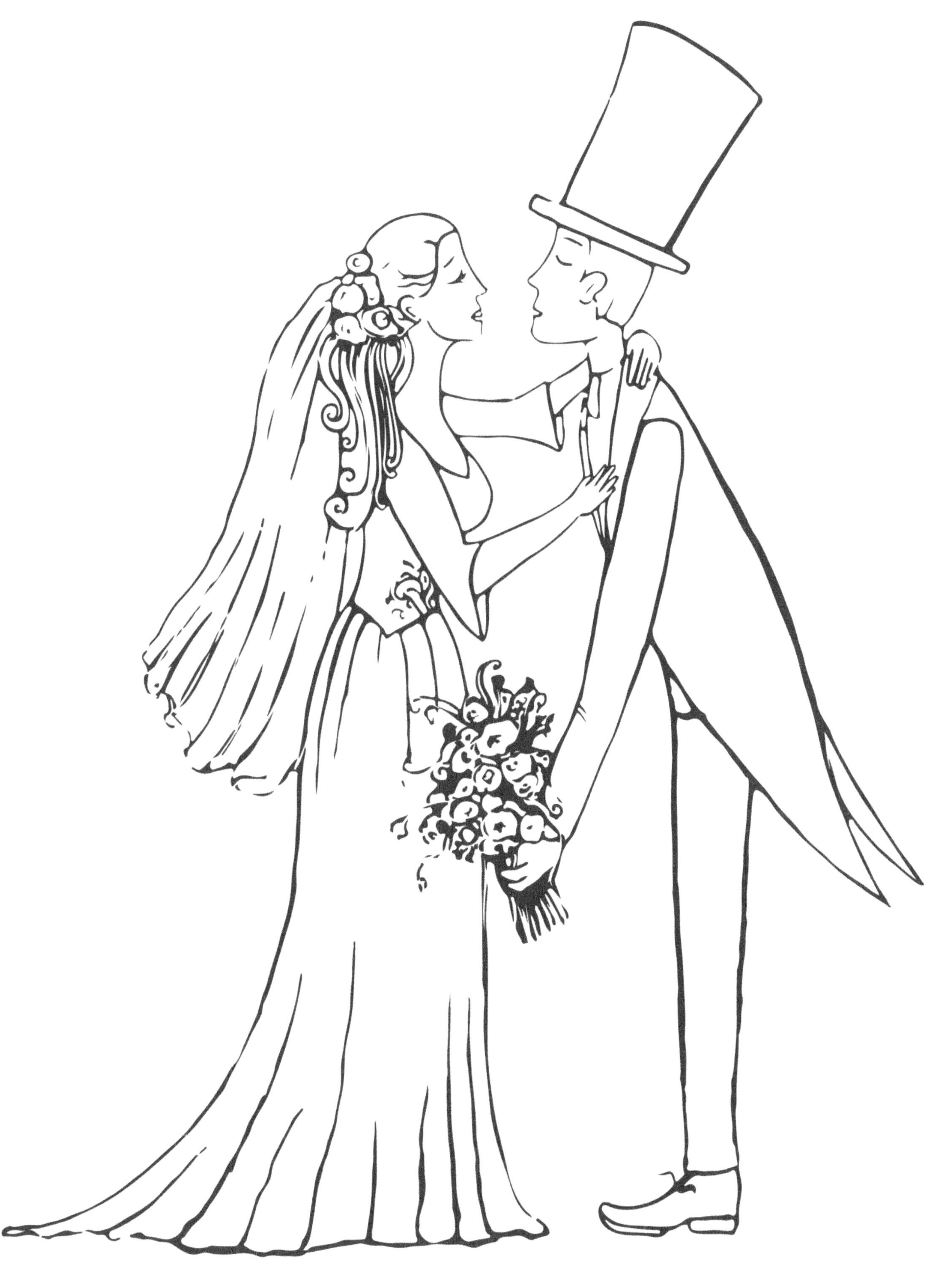

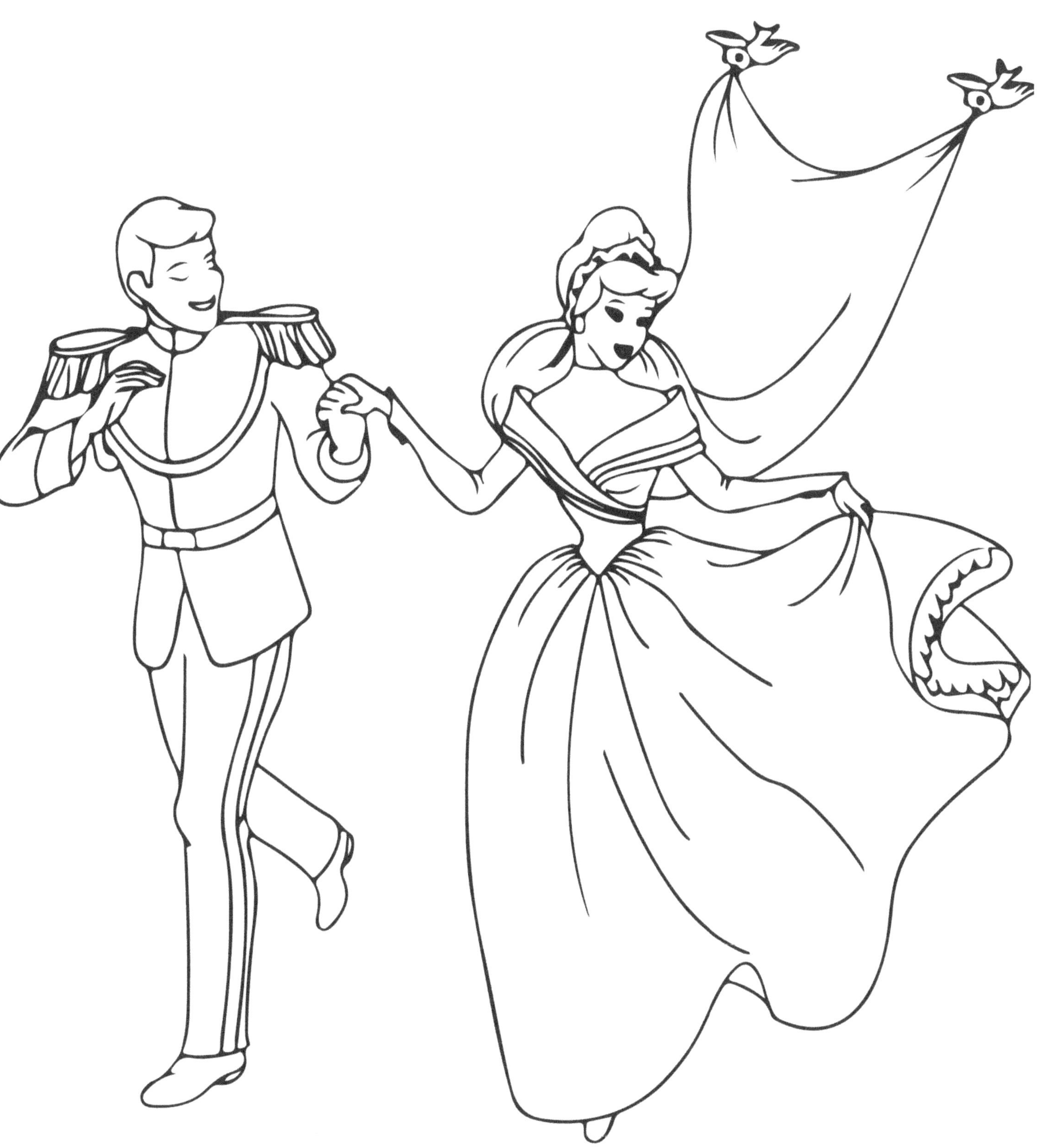

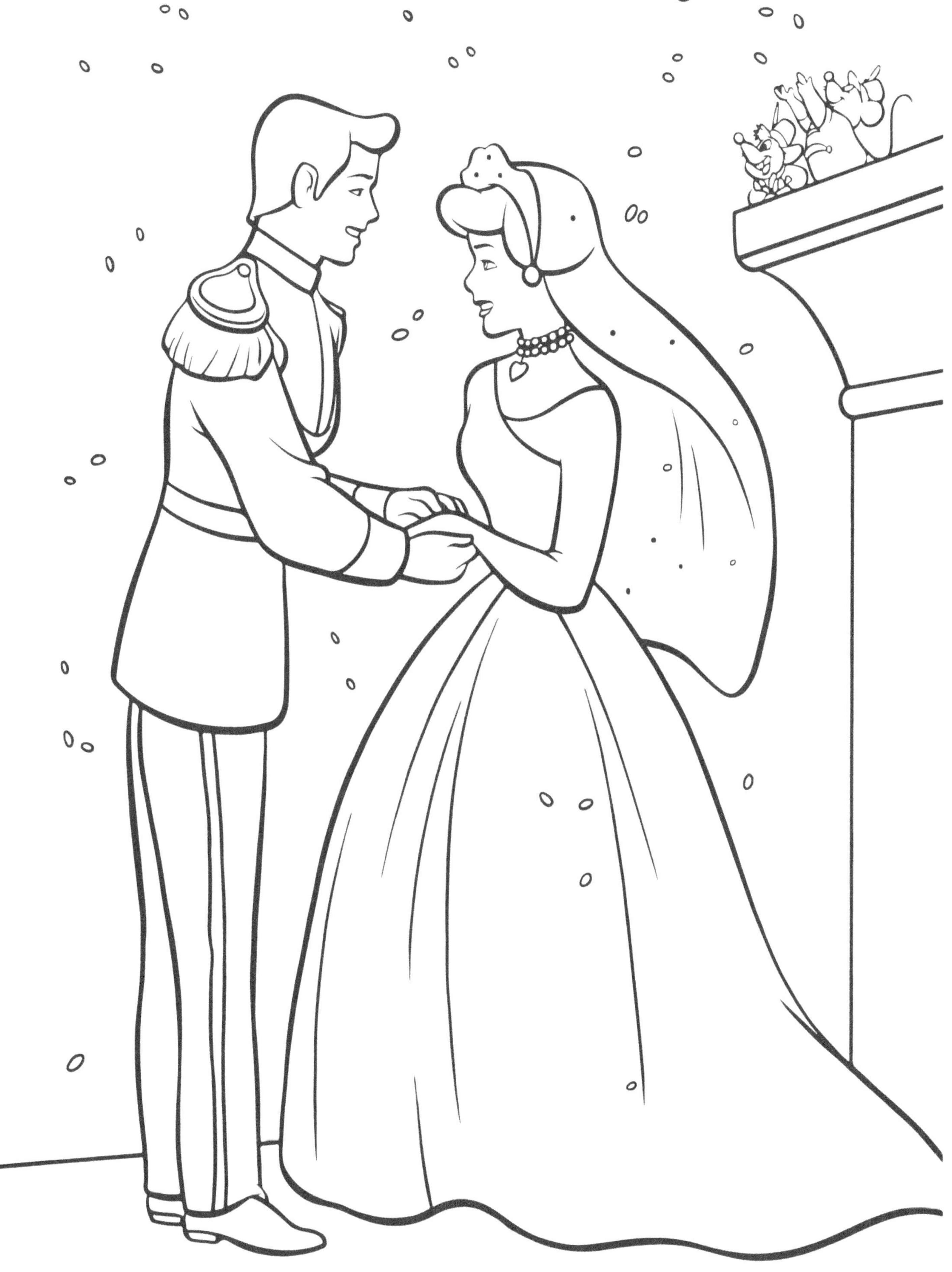

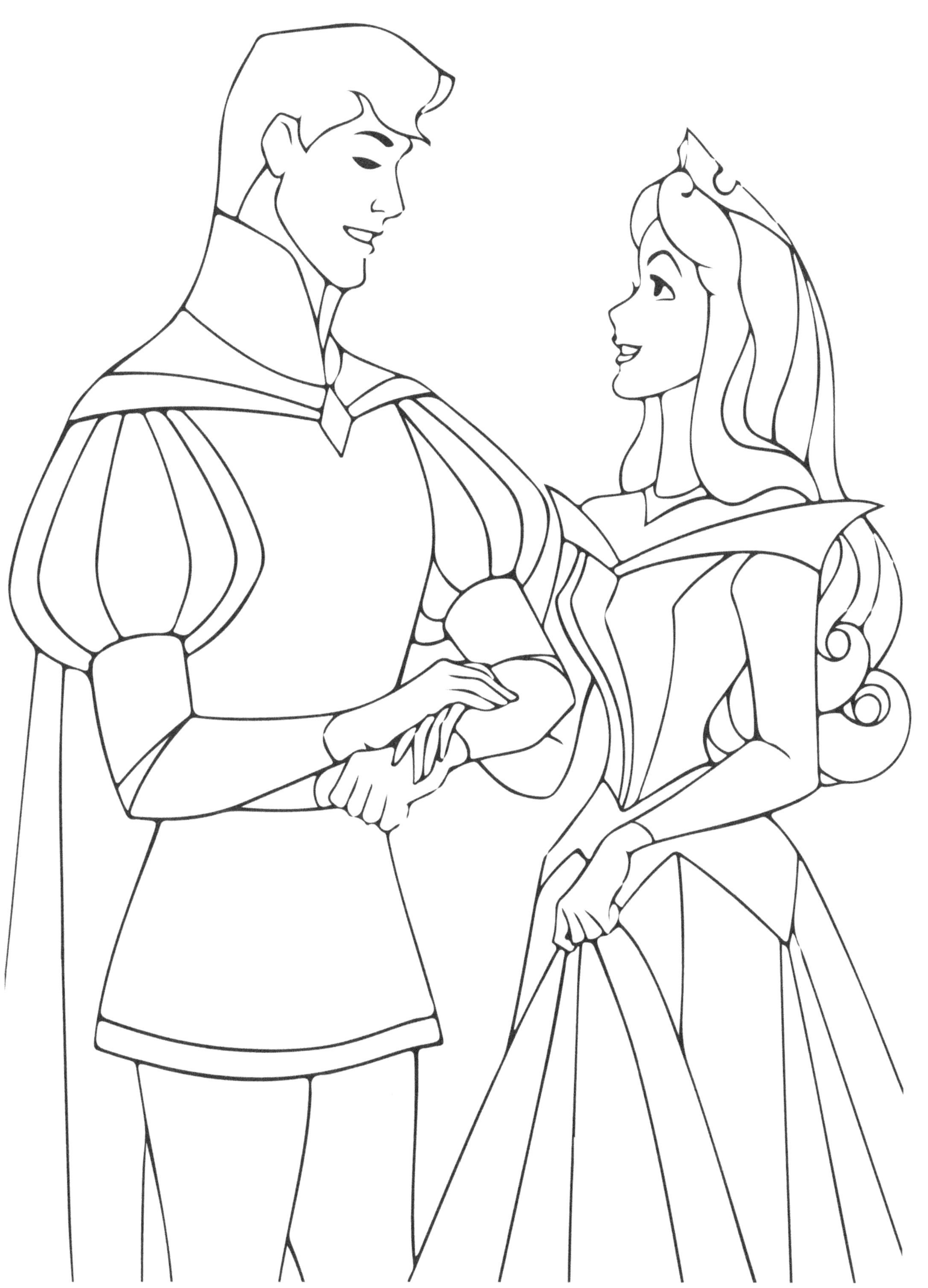

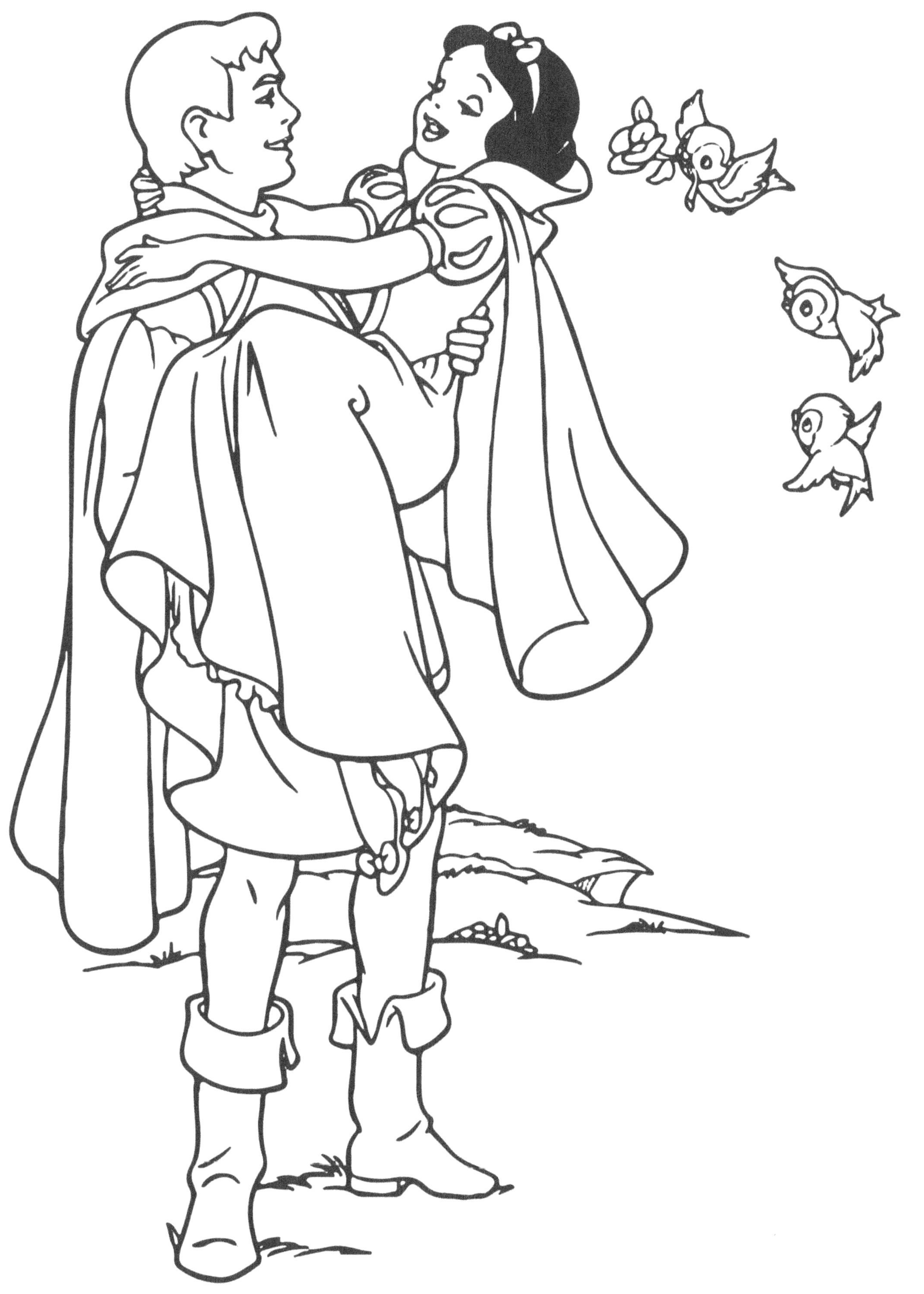

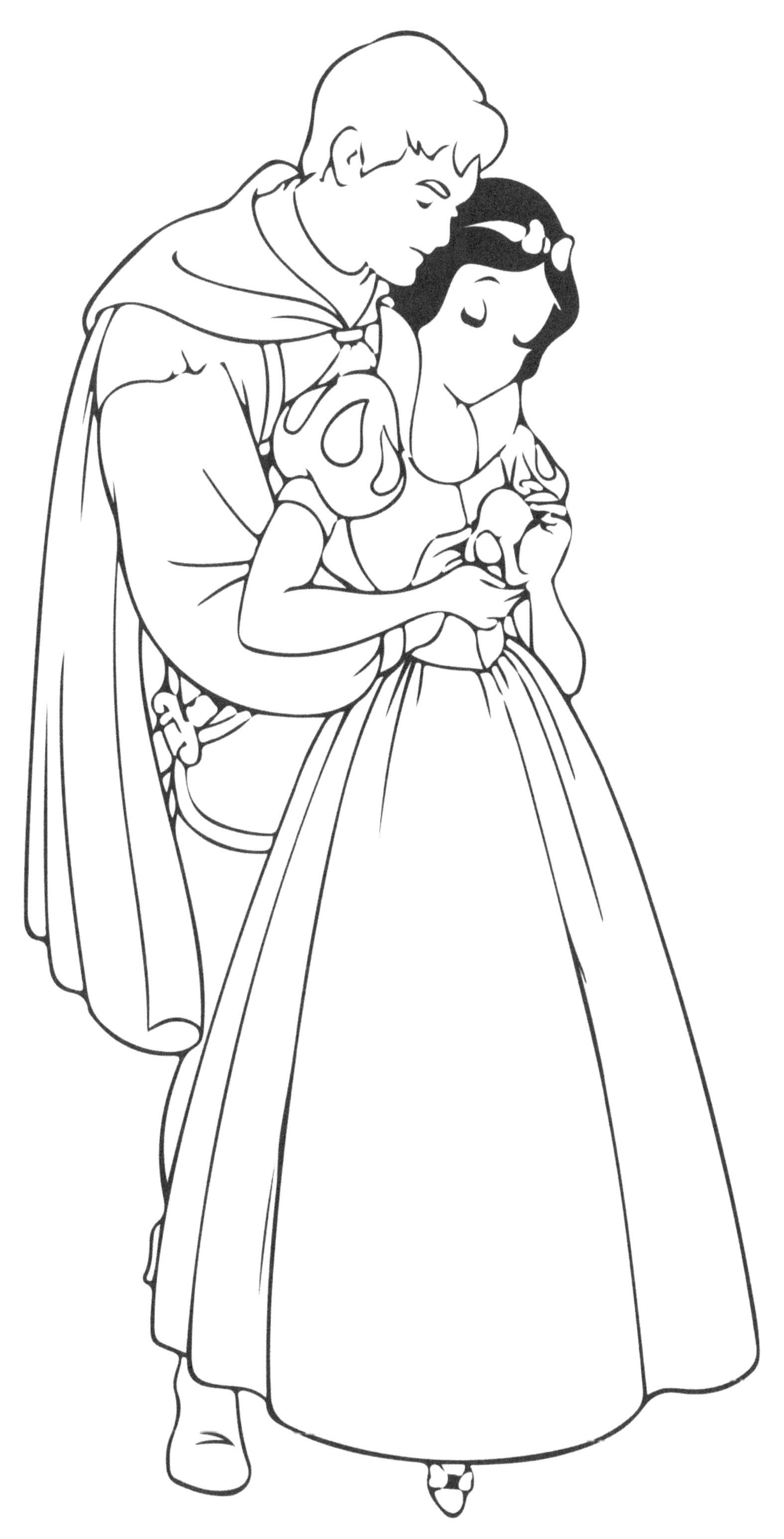

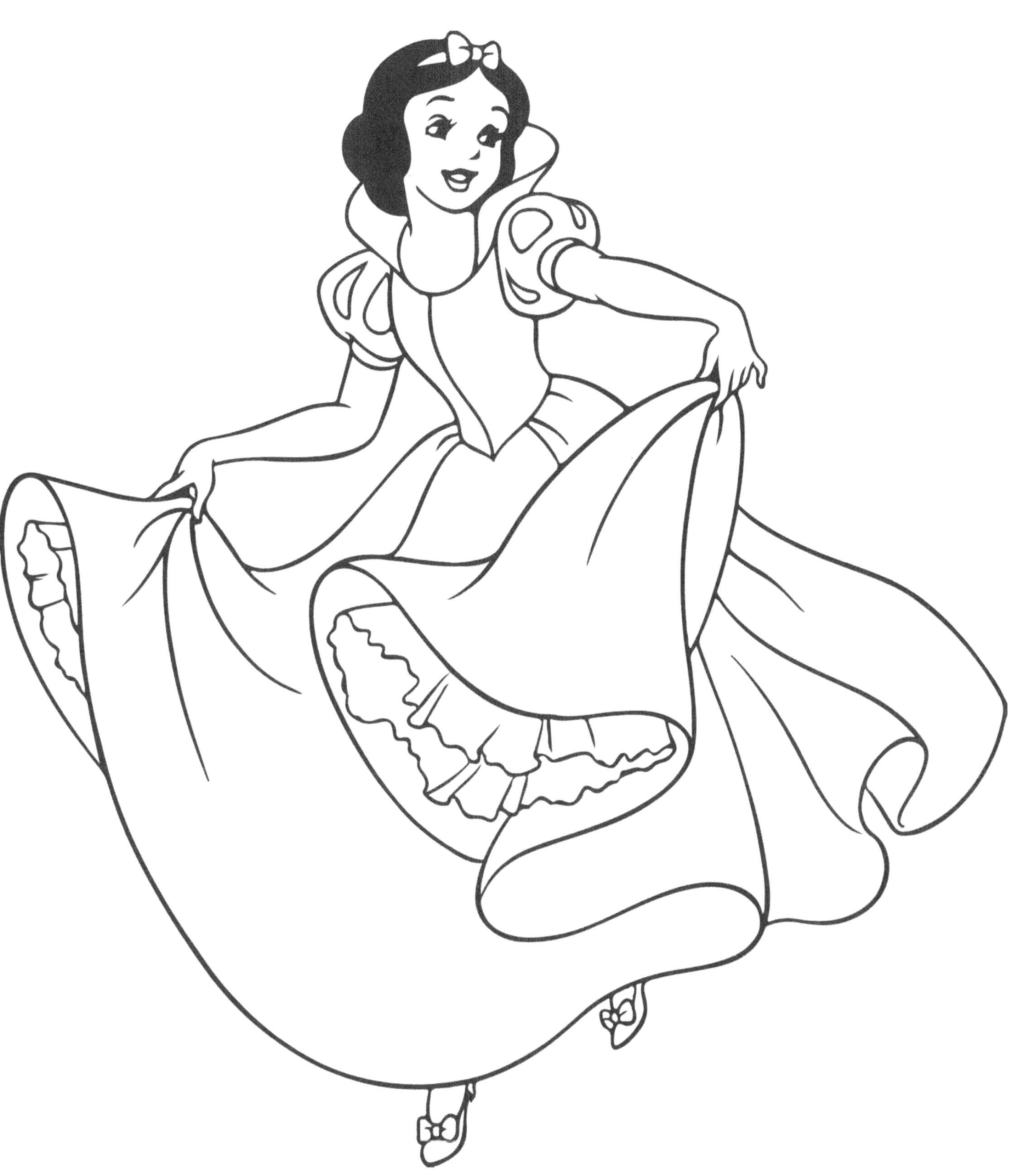

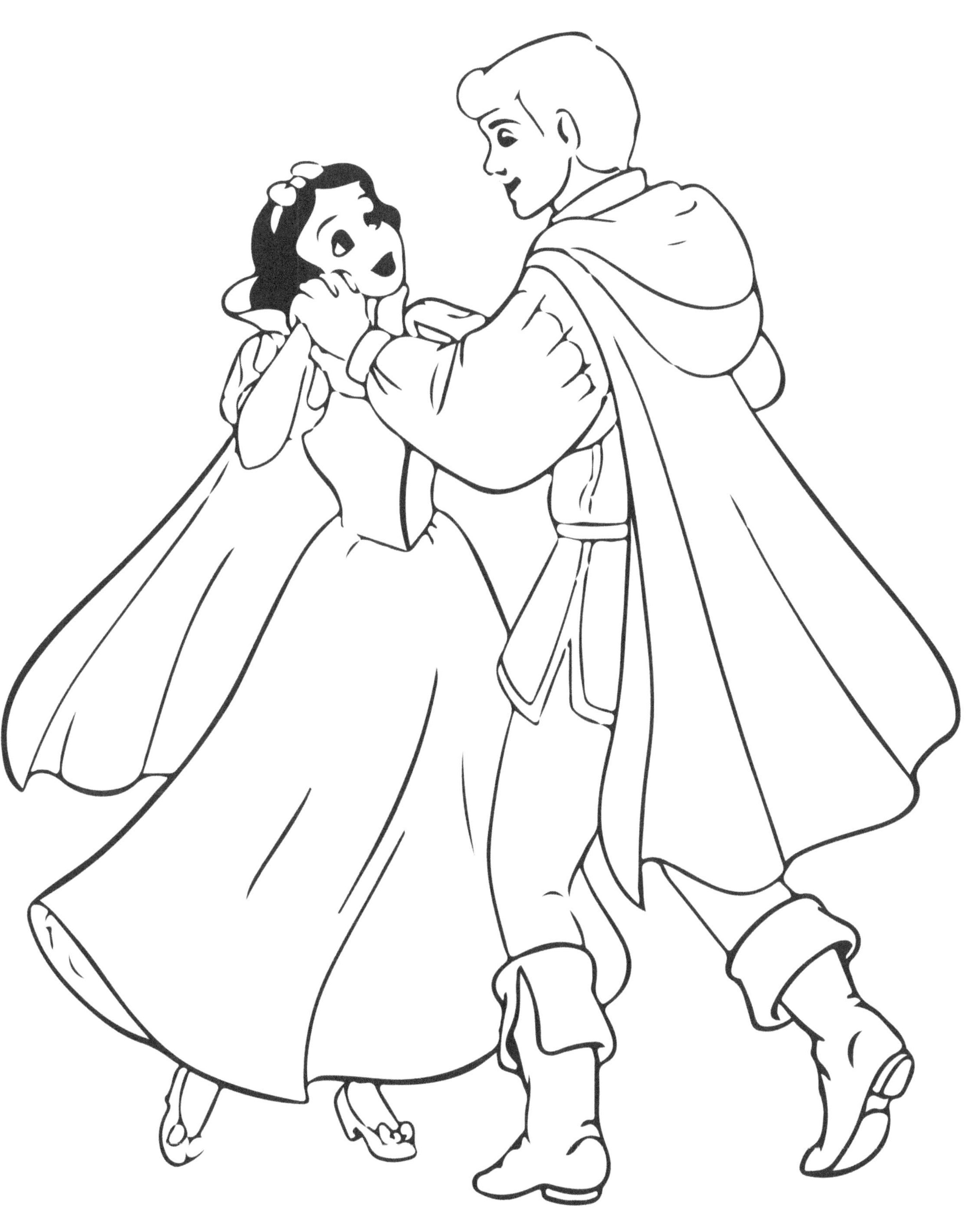